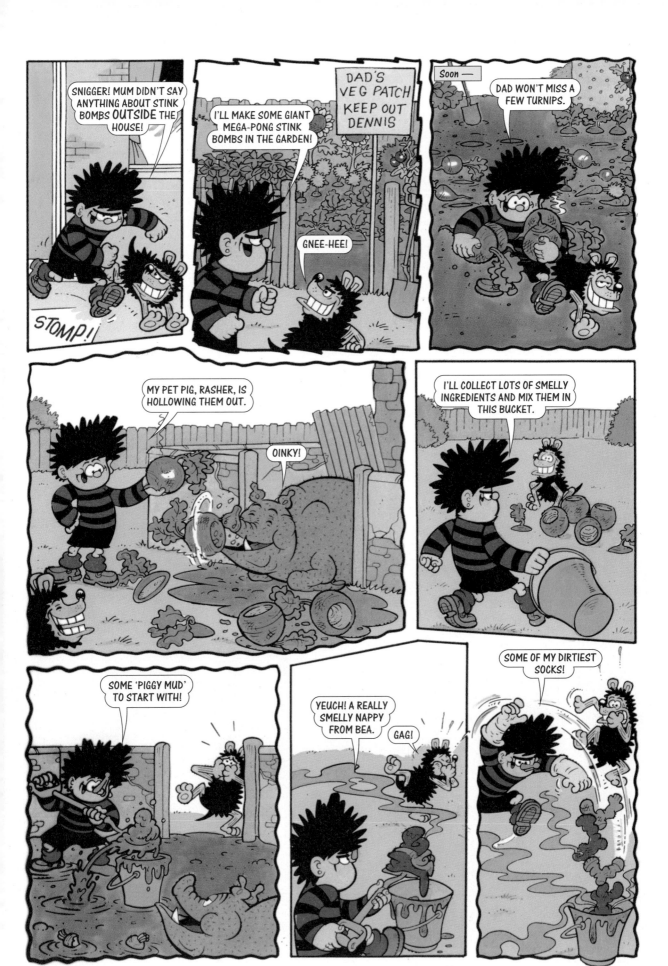

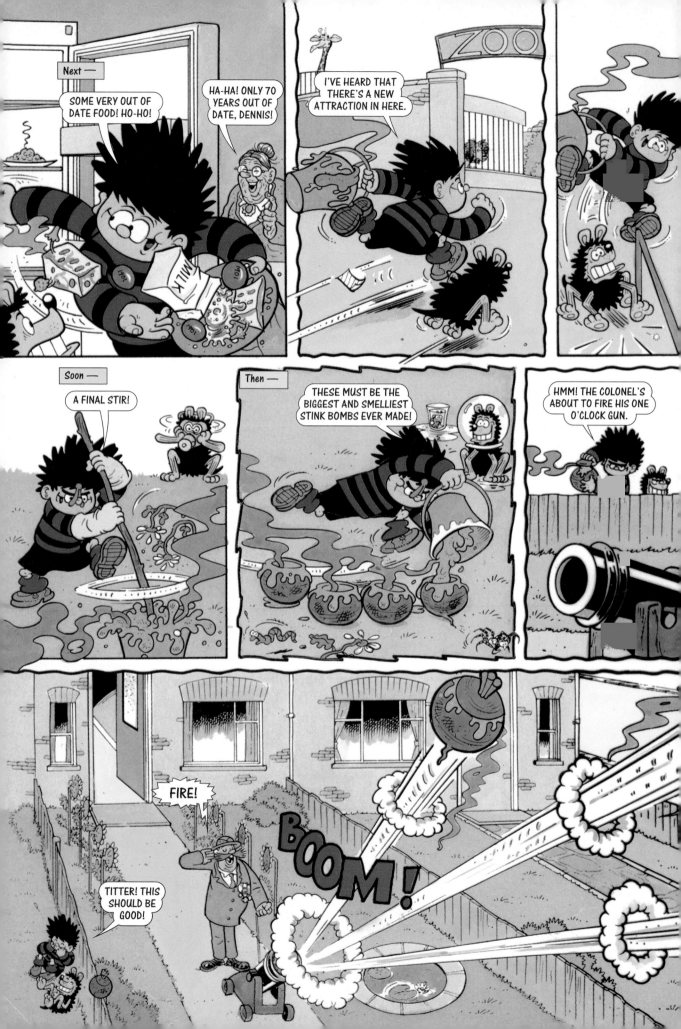

Safari so good!

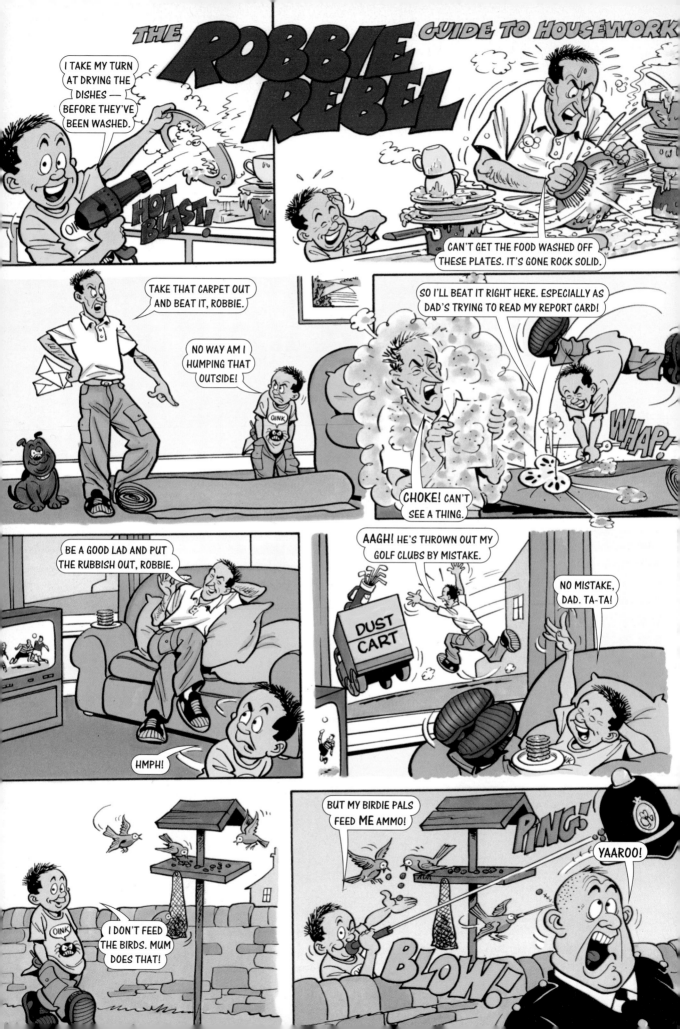

GROAN! WHERE AM I? WHAT HAPPENED?

LUCKILY, YOUR RIDING HAT TOOK MOST OF THE IMPACT.

WHAT'S HAPPENED, MOONFLOWER?

HE HAD A FALL. LET'S TAKE HIM TO OUR CAMP, MUM.

At the New Age camp —

MUM'LL KNOW WHAT TO DO.

Within minutes —

IT'S ALL BECOMING CLEAR AGAIN — I THINK! HUH?

CHUCKLE! HE MUST THINK HIS EYES ARE PLAYING TRICKS ON HIM.

YOU'RE A BETTER-LOOKING GENERAL JUMBO THAN ME, MOONFLOWER.

Next day —

MY DAD SAYS YOU CAN STAY ON OUR LAND AS LONG AS YOU LIKE.

HEH! LOOKS LIKE FLOWER POWER WINS THE DAY!

JUMBO

GNASHER and GNIPPER

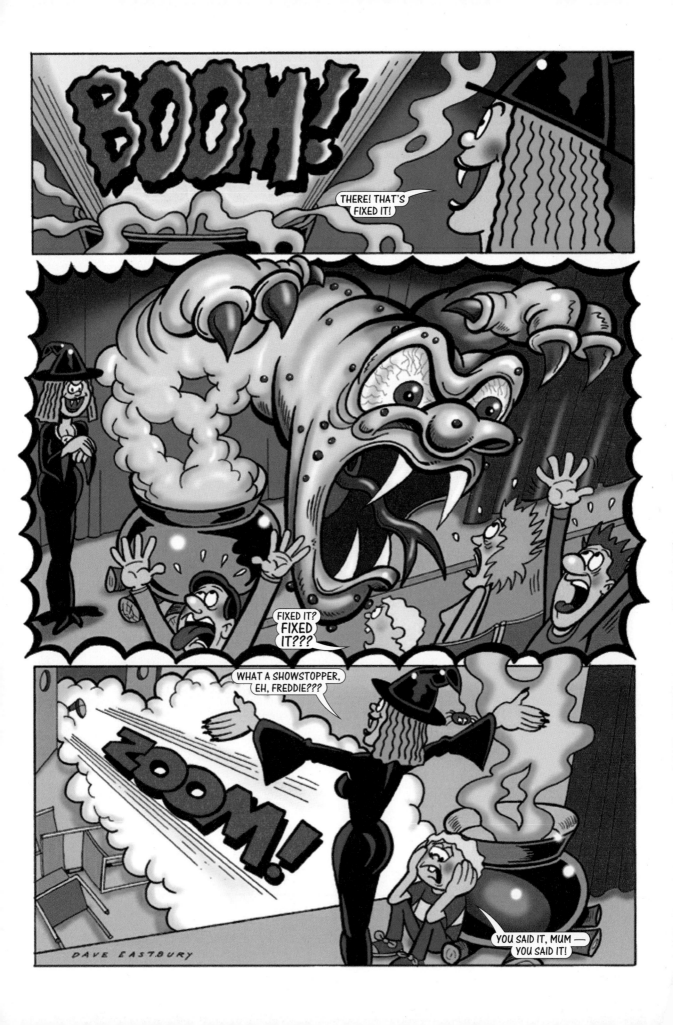

Safari so good!

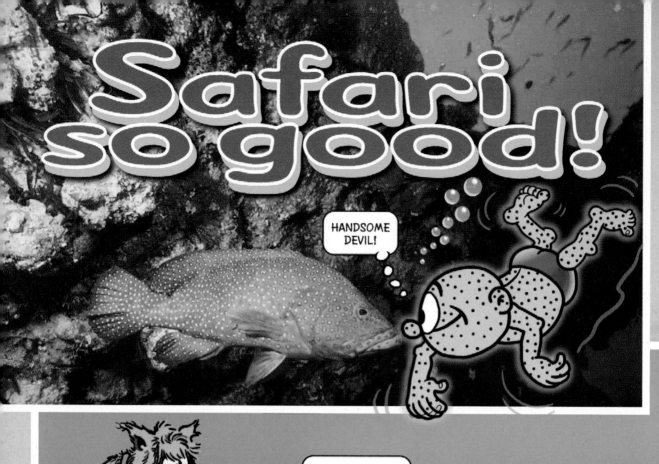

THE NUMSKULLS

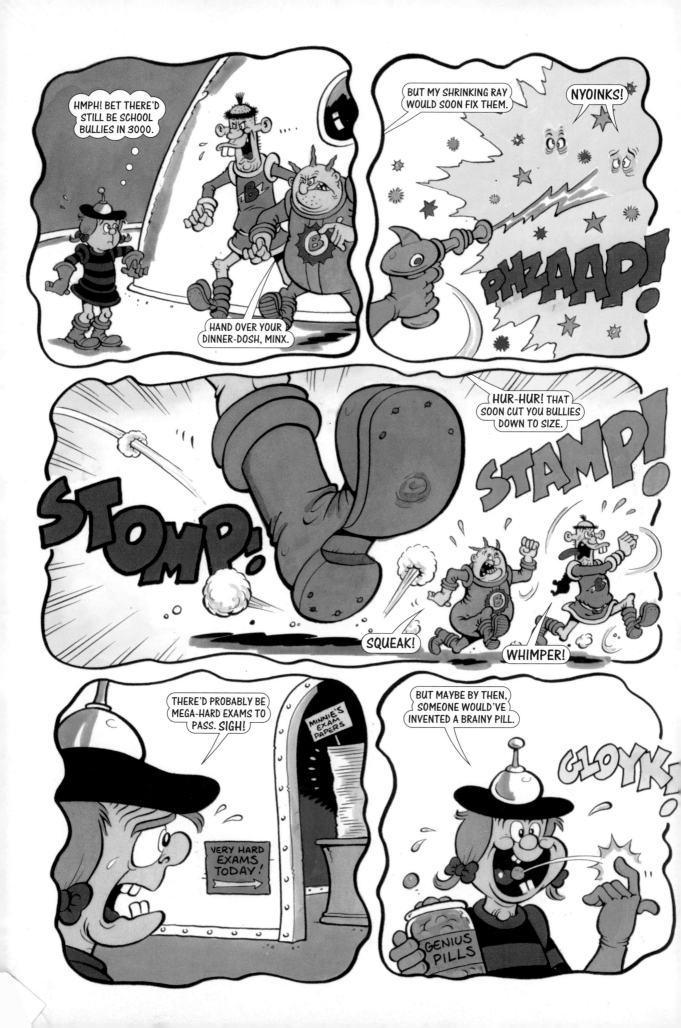

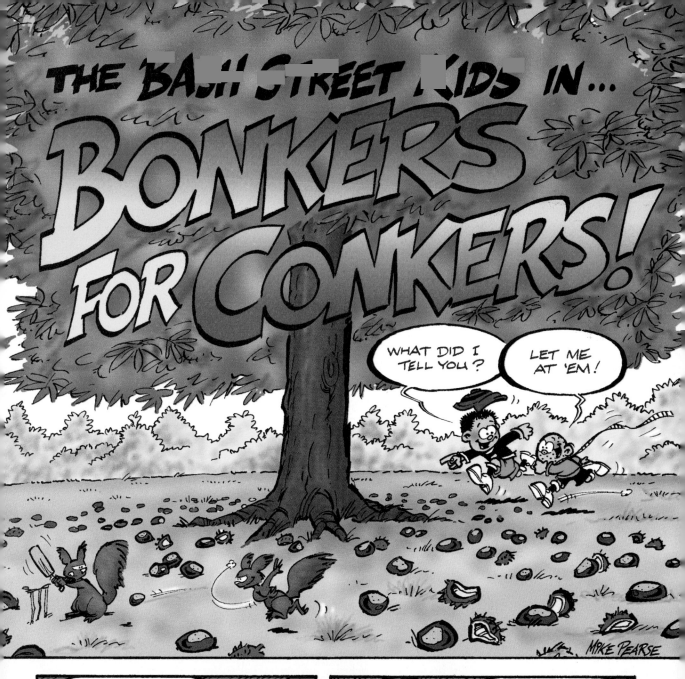

AND SO...

RIGHT! DOES EVERY-ONE HAVE THEIR CONKERS?

YUP!

YUP!

YUPPITY-YUP!

HOW IS THIS GOING TO TEACH US MATHS?

WHO CARES?

NOW, I'VE PUT ALL YOUR NAMES IN MY HAT, SO THE MATCHES WILL BE CHOSEN AT RANDOM.

PLUG

SMIFFY, COULD YOU PICK OUT TWO NAMES, PLEASE?

TWO.

NOW THAT'S ...ER...

ON SECOND THOUGHTS, PERHAPS WILFRED COULD DO THE HONOURS...

SO THE FIRST NAME IS ... SPOTTY!

OH, YEAH!

AND HE WILL PLAY AGAINST...

...CUTHBERT!

OH, NO!

④

9

11

OKAY, BEFORE THE FINAL, LET'S HAVE A SHORT BREAK.

"DANNY ... CHAMPION OF THE WORLD!" THAT HAS A NICE RING TO IT!

I PREFER: "DANNY... BEATEN BY CUTHBERT!"

YEAH!

WELL, YOU BOTH KNOW ALL ABOUT THAT, DON'T YOU?

GRRRRRR...!

NUDGE!

IF DANNY'S HEAD GETS ANY BIGGER HE WON'T BE ABLE TO STAND UP STRAIGHT!

BUT WHAT CAN WE DO ABOUT IT?

I'VE GOT AN IDEA!

AND SO ...

RIGHT, ARE WE READY FOR ...?

WHAT ON EARTH IS GOING ON?!

12

SURE ENOUGH, ONE WEEK LATER ...

AND THEN, "SMACK-A-ROO", CUTHBERT'S CONKER WAS HISTORY!

REALLY...

HOW FASCINATING...

AND THIS WAS THE TREE WHERE SPOTTY AND I FIRST GOT THE CONKERS!

DANNY'S EPIC STORY BEGAN RIGHT HERE!

YEAH ... STUPID TREE...!

KICK!

BOM!

BOM! BOM!

BOM!

BOM!

!

BOM!

BOM!

WELL, WHAT D'YOU KNOW ...?

...THE FINAL WINNER HAS TURNED OUT TO BE THE CONKERS!

THE END

Safari so good!

BILLY the CAT

SCHOOLBOY WILLIAM GRANGE, SECRETLY THE ACROBATIC CRIME FIGHTER, BILLY THE CAT, RETURNS TO MARHAM AFTER A HOLIDAY ABROAD —

WOW! IT'S ALL BEEN HAPPENING WHILE I'VE BEEN AWAY.

CRIME WAVE GROWS...

...WHERE IS BILLY THE CAT?

£100 REWARD FOR PIC OF MYSTERY MAN- IS CAPTAIN FANTASTIC AN URBAN MYTH?

SOON —

WAHEY! IT'S GREAT TO BE IN ACTION AGAIN! MY GUESS IS THAT THE CRIME WAVE IS DOWN TO A GANG CALLED "THE ACES".

BILLY IS HEADING FOR THE ACES' HIDEOUT —

LOOK OUT, ACES! THE CAT IS ON THE PROWL.

BINGO! TWO ACES UP TO NO GOOD. I'LL SHADOW THEM.

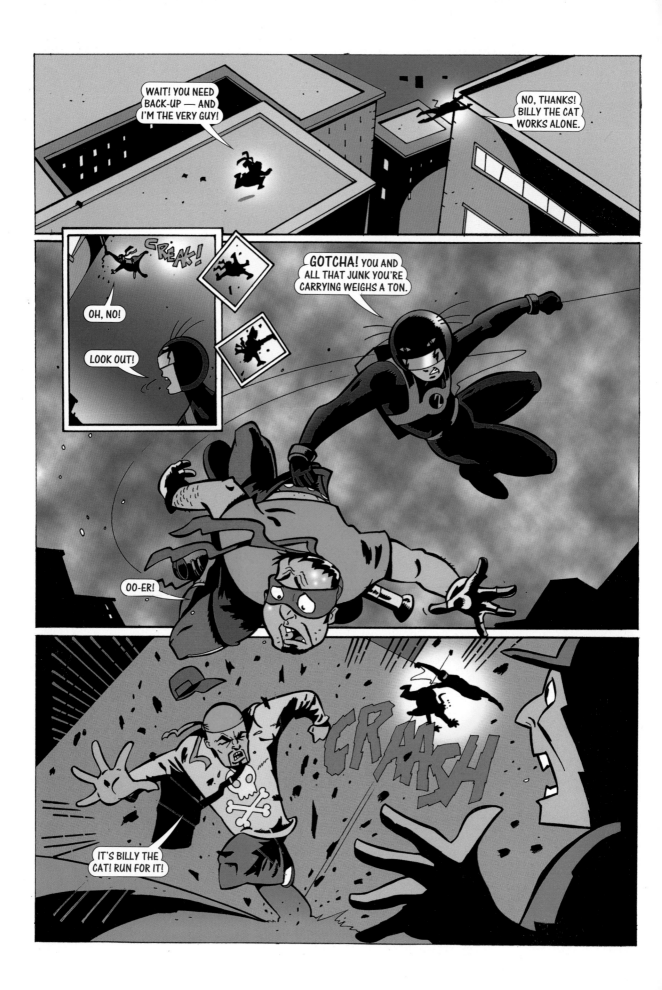

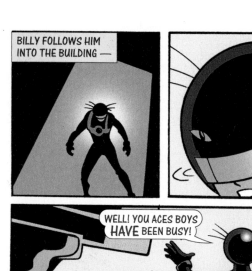

BILLY FOLLOWS HIM
INTO THE BUILDING —

CLICK

LOOKS LIKE WE'VE
CAUGHT OURSELVES
A SNOOPER.

WELL! YOU ACES BOYS
HAVE BEEN BUSY!

ACES RULE

YOU'RE GONNA REGRET POKING
YOUR WHISKERS IN HERE.

BUT, AT THAT
MOMENT, UP ABOVE —

BILLY WENT THIS WAY.
I'LL . . . WHAAAAA!

CRASSHHH!

YEEAARGH!

WHAT THE — ?

CRIPES!

DEM SOFTIES WANT FAIRIES. DEM SOFTIES GONNA **GET** FAIRIES!

GNU-HUH?

ME KNEW MY BUMBLE BEE COZZIE FER 'AT FANCY DRESS PARTY WOULD COME IN 'ANDY!

GLOO

WHERE IZZIT?

GNEH?

GOTTIT! DIS IS WOT ME WOZ AFTER! CHRISSYMAS TREE STAR.

DERE! ME'S GOTTA FAIRY WAND!

CLEANEST SHIRT AWARD 1996

DAD'S BEST POOL CUE— (ONLY ONE NOT RIPPED THE CLOTH)

AN GOOD OL' GNASHER HAS DUG A SEKRET TUNNEL INTO DA SOFTIES' GARDEN.

MENACES in SPACE
HA-HA! YOU ALMOST GOT ME, GNASHER!
GNEE-HEE!
STARRING—
DENNIS and GNASHER

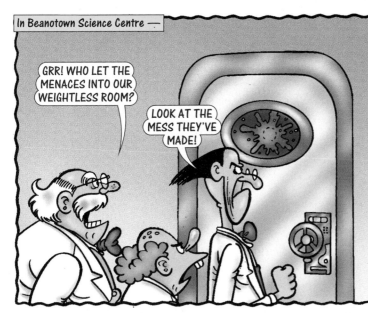

In Beanotown Science Centre —

GRR! WHO LET THE MENACES INTO OUR WEIGHTLESS ROOM?

LOOK AT THE MESS THEY'VE MADE!

RZZP!

SPLAT!

I'LL FIX THEM!

CLICK!

OFF

And —

THAT'S BROUGHT THEM DOWN TO EARTH WITH A BUMP!

HAW-HAW!

ZONK!

THUD!

HUH! SPOILSPORTS! WE WERE ENJOYING THAT!

Next —

WALKING BOOTS? WHAT'S SO SPECIAL ABOUT THEM?

WALKING BOOTS

GNO IDEA.

GNASHER and GNIPPER

SIGH! WE NEVER HAVE ANY VISITORS TO OUR HOUSE.

GRR! YOU TWO CHASE PEOPLE AWAY BEFORE THEY REACH THE FRONT DOOR!

GNEE HEE!

WAA!

GNASH! GNIP!

HELP!

OR YOU HASSLE VISITORS WHEN I SERVE TEA!

OO . . . ER!

SCOFF!

CHOMP!

HUMPH! ALL YOUR FAULT OUR HOUSE IS SO QUIET!

PESKY DOGS!

Outside —

THEY WANT VISITORS — THEY'LL GET VISITORS!

NUDGE!

NOVELTY ROAD RUNNERS THIS WAY

HEH-HEH! THIS'LL DO THE TRICK!

Soon —

VISITORS!

ER?

YEE-HAR!

WHAT'S GOING ON?

CLUMP!

HOLD ON! LOOK AT THE MESS OF MY CARPET!

PUFF!

PANT!

SHE'S NEVER PLEASED!

THE 3 BEARS

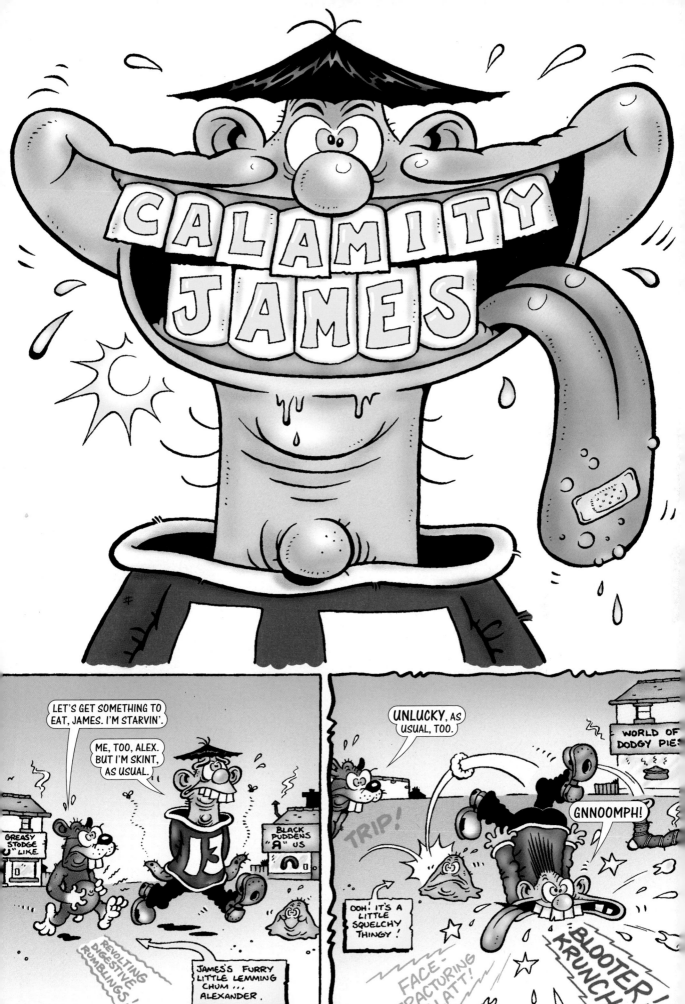

GOT A TASTE FOR THE GREAT
CHARACTERS IN THIS ANNUAL?...

WILFRID   DANNY   SMIFFY   PLUG   FATTY   SPOTTY   SIDNEY   TOOTS   'ERBERT

THE BASH STREET KIDS in TREASURE

EIGHT . . . NINE . . . TEN, HALT!

OOF!

BAH! THERE'S A BIT OF THE MAP MISSING. HMM! IT SAYS TO WALK FIVE PACES AND DIG FOR THE TREASURE . . . BUT IN WHICH DIRECTION?

LOOK! A MOLE! OUCH!

TITTER! IT THOUGHT YOUR NOSE WAS A BERRY!

BITE!

HMM! I WONDER WHAT THIS IS?

DELIVER TO ME TEN PACKETS OF CHOCCY BICCIES . . . EH? WHAT?

HA-HA! SIDNEY'S FOUND HEAD'S PHONE CABLE!

TUG!

GRR! WHY DID YOU DO THAT, SMIFFY?

ALL OF THE COINS WERE LIKE THIS . . . WAY PAST THEIR SELL BY DATE!

WAH!

BAH! IDIOT!